TURTLES

Patricia Davis

Grolier
an imprint of

SCHOLASTIC

www.scholastic.com/librarypublishing

Published 2008 by Grolier
An imprint of Scholastic Library Publishing
Old Sherman Turnpike, Danbury,
Connecticut 06816

For The Brown Reference Group plc
Project Editor: Jolyon Goddard
Copy-editors: Ann Baggaley, Leon Gray
Picture Researcher: Clare Newman
Designers: Jeni Child, Lynne Ross,
        Sarah Williams
Managing Editor: Bridget Giles

Volume ISBN-13: 978-0-7172-6288-5
Volume ISBN-10: 0-7172-6288-X

**Library of Congress
Cataloging-in-Publication Data**

Nature's children. Set 3.
     p. cm.
  Includes bibliographical references and
index.
  ISBN 13: 978-0-7172-8082-7
  ISBN 10: 0-7172-8082-9
  1. Animals--Encyclopedias, Juvenile. I.
  Grolier Educational (Firm)
  QL49.N384 2008
  590.3--dc22
                        2007031568

Printed and bound in China

Contents

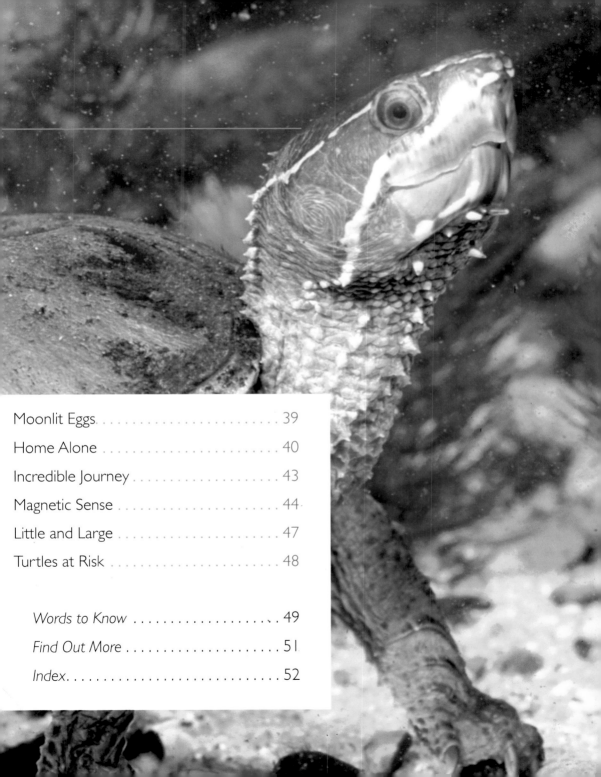

FACT FILE: Turtles

Class	Reptiles (Reptilia)
Order	Turtles, tortoises, and terrapins (Testudines or Chelonia)
Families	12 main families; the largest in North America is the subaquatic turtle family (Emydidae)
Genera	90 genera; 20 genera occur naturally in North America
Species	About 250 species worldwide; 50 species can be found in North America
World distribution	All the continents except Antarctica
Habitat	Some species live on land; some in seas and oceans; others in streams, lakes, and ponds
Distinctive physical characteristics	Body covered with a protective shell; four limbs; hard, toothless beak
Habits	Lay eggs on land, buried in sand, soil, or mud; parents do not look after their young
Diet	Varies with species

Introduction

Turtles first appeared on Earth about 200 million years ago. Perhaps the main reason for their success is their shells. These hard, bony structures are a safe haven in times of danger. Turtles live in many places, or habitats: on land, in streams, rivers, lakes, and ponds, and in the sea. Some turtles can live more than 100 years. Today, many turtles are endangered animals. People must do everything in their power to preserve these truly amazing animals.

The red-footed tortoise makes a popular pet.

The eastern painted turtle has colorful patterns on the underside of its shell.

6

Reptilian Relations

Turtles are **reptiles**. Other reptiles include crocodiles, lizards, and snakes. Reptiles share many common features. Some reptiles spend a lot of time in water, but they all need to breathe air. Reptiles have another feature in common: they are all cold-blooded. That means they cannot control their body temperature.

The human body stays at more or less the same temperature no matter how hot or cold it is. **Mammals** have fur to keep warm. Reptiles do not have fur. Instead, they have a thick scaly or leathery covering. A reptile's body gets cooler when it moves into the shade. Its body warms up when it moves back into the sun.

Sun Seekers

Turtles live any place that has warm temperatures for at least part of the year. Although turtles can survive very cold winters, they need plenty of sunshine in summer.

In North America, turtles live throughout the United States and Mexico, but only in the southern part of Canada. The northern part of Canada is too cold. Some turtles, such as snapping turtles, can be found in many parts of the United States. Other turtles live within a smaller area. For example, the yellow-blotched map turtle lives in a small area near the Mississippi River.

A common
snapping turtle
basks on a log
beside a lake.

Giant tortoises
live on tropical
islands such as
the Galápagos
and Mauritius.

What's in a Name?

Turtles may be called **tortoises** or **terrapins** depending on where they live. Tortoises live only on the land and are poor swimmers. Most tortoises live near desert or grassland. They have stumpy legs with high, rounded shells.

Terrapins are common in North America. They spend some of their time on land and the rest of their time in freshwater streams, lakes, and ponds. Their shell varies in shape, depending on the **species**. Their feet usually end with sharp claws. Terrapins that spend a lot of time in the water may have webbed feet.

Sea turtles live in the Atlantic and Pacific oceans and in the Gulf of Mexico. They have flattened, paddlelike legs that are perfect for swimming. Sea turtles spend most of their lives in the sea and only come ashore to lay their eggs. Some sea turtles are huge compared to tortoises and terrapins.

Living Armor

All turtles have a protective shell to guard against **predators**. Turtles move slowly and cannot run away from predators. Instead, the turtle pulls its head, tail, and legs into its shell. If danger is near, it will do so very quickly.

The shape of the shell can reveal how a turtle lives. Some shells are smooth and streamlined. This type of shell is designed to glide through water and might belong to a sea turtle or terrapin. Tortoise shells are usually high and domed, which makes it hard for predators to crush them between their jaws. One exception is the African pancake tortoise, which has a flat, flexible shell. This tortoise can squeeze into cracks between rocks and hide from predators.

Turtle shells have different colors. Some are black, brown, green, or a mixture of dull colors. Other shells have brightly colored dots, streaks, or patterns. The Eastern painted turtle is one of the most colorful turtles. It has a has a black, red, and yellow shell.

The faint yellow lines on the upper surface of the shell give the map turtle its name.

13

Like all box turtles, the plastron of the three-toed box turtle is hinged so it can close its shell tightly to avoid predators.

Top and Bottom

A turtle's shell is made up of two parts. The top part is called the **carapace**, and the underside is called the **plastron**. The two parts of the shell are usually connected by bony ridges. The turtle's head, stocky legs, and tail poke out of holes between the carapace and plastron.

Tough, horny scales, called **scutes**, cover the outer layer of the shell of a tortoise. Sometimes the scutes are lumpy or pointed and help the turtle blend in with its surroundings or look threatening. Not all turtles have scutes. The shell of the leatherback sea turtle is soft and leathery.

The inner layer of a turtle's shell consists of about 60 **bones**. These bones are connected to the turtle's backbone, so the animal can never crawl out of its shell.

Shedding Skin

Like their close relatives the snakes, sea turtles and terrapins shed their **skin**. Snakes shed their skin in one go, but turtles shed their skin all the time in pieces. Sometimes a turtle will help the shedding process by rubbing its body against a stone.

Tortoises also shed their skin, but most of it turns into scutes. This offers added protection against predators. It also explains why the shell of a tortoise is much heavier than that of a sea turtle or terrapin. It is possible to estimate the age of a tortoise by counting the rings formed on the scutes as they grow. This method is not very accurate, however, since the scutes fall off the shell over time.

The skin of the yellow-blotched map turtle is dark green with yellow stripes. There is a yellow dot behind each eye.

The stinkpot is a small turtle with a pungent smell.

18

Stink Bomb

Most adult turtles have a strong shell to protect
them. However, some turtles are very small,
and the shell might not be enough to deter
a hungry predator. Fortunately, some small
turtles have developed another form of defense.
The stinkpot, mud turtle, and musk turtle
have two sacs, called glands, that produce a
foul-smelling liquid called **musk**. When these
tiny turtles feel threatened, they squirt musk
all over their attacker. So the stinkpot really
does live up to its name!

Turtle Senses

At night, turtles have good eyesight. That helps them look for food in the dark. During the day, their vision is not so good, and they cannot see colors very well. Turtles that spend a lot of time in water, such as the snapping turtles, have eyes near the top of their head. These turtles hide under the surface of the water, keeping the eyes and nostrils above water. Turtles also have protective eyelids. Unlike snakes, turtles can blink.

Instead of ears that stick out like a dog or cat, turtles have two small openings on either side of their head. The openings are covered by skin, but the turtle can still hear well.

Turtles smell their surroundings by noisily gulping air into their mouth. A hungry turtle will sniff out food in this way.

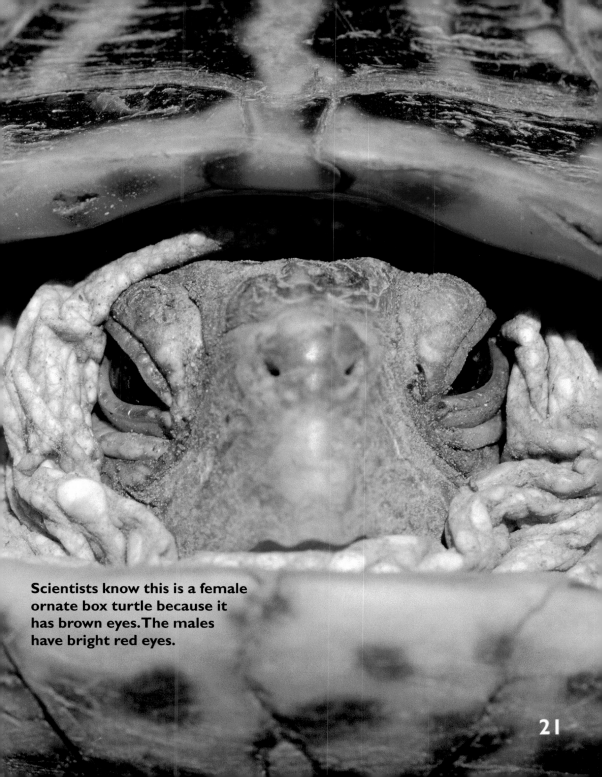

Scientists know this is a female ornate box turtle because it has brown eyes. The males have bright red eyes.

A loggerhead turtle devours a spiny lobster in the warm waters of the North Atlantic.

Varied Diets

Hungry turtles eat a range of different foods. Some turtles, especially the tortoises, are **herbivores** and mainly eat plants. Others are **carnivores** and mainly eat meat. The snapping turtle is a carnivore. It loves to eat crayfish, crabs, fish, frogs, snakes, birds' eggs, and insects.

Most turtles are **omnivores** and eat just about anything. Many turtles have favorite foods. Leatherback turtles love to eat jellyfish, while the yellow-blotched map turtle prefers insects.

Many turtles can last days, or even weeks, without food when there is little available. When food is plentiful, however, turtles often gorge themselves until they are fat.

Toothless Turtles

Most animals use teeth to chop and grind up food before swallowing it. Turtles don't have teeth. Instead they have a hard beak with a jagged cutting edge. The beaks of some turtles are sharp. The snapping turtle can easily cut a fish in two. As well as the beak, a turtle has a tongue to slide food around its mouth and down its throat.

The alligator snapping turtle has a pinkish growth in its mouth. When the turtle is hungry, it opens its mouth and waves the pink growth around to resemble a worm. That attracts fish into the turtle's mouth. Once the fish is inside the turtle's mouth, the turtle's jaws snap shut!

Slow Coach

Turtles are well known for being slow. The land-dwelling tortoises have short, stubby legs and small feet, which prevent them from moving quickly. Even terrapins can move faster than most tortoises. Some terrapins can even climb. For example, the agile stinkpot can crawl up small trees.

All sea turtles and most terrapins move better in water than they do on land. They can glide through water quickly. Large sea turtles swim hundreds of miles to search for food or nesting sites.

Their legs may move slowly, but carnivorous turtles can move their head quickly and snap their jaws closed at lightning speed. It takes a snapping turtle less than one-tenth of a second to close its jaws around an unsuspecting fish!

The green turtle has
a streamlined shell and
huge paddlelike flippers.

Turtle Lungs

A turtle uses its mouth, nose, and lungs to breath. Turtles that spend a lot of time in the water can also absorb small amounts of oxygen directly from the water. Others have a tall snorkel-like nose that pokes out of the water while they swim below the surface. Turtles can also slow down their heartbeat when they are underwater so their body needs less oxygen.

A turtle's lungs are different from a person's lungs. When a human breathes in, the ribcage expands to fill the lungs with air. As the lungs deflate, the ribcage contracts to empty the lungs of air. A turtle's ribcage cannot expand and contract in this way because it is fixed to its shell. Instead, a turtle is able to fill its lungs with air by simply moving its limbs.

Aquatic turtles must surface at regular intervals to take fresh air into their lungs.

A spiny softshell turtle basks on a patch of leaves to keep warm. These turtles are never far from water.

Hot and Cold

Turtles cannot control their body temperature. Instead, they spend many hours a day basking in the sunshine. Turtles can overheat, though, so they prefer to stay near the shade or water. Desert turtles struggle to find shady places in which to cool down. When no shade can be found, these turtles dig holes in the sand, where it is much cooler. If the weather gets too hot, the turtle may decide to spend the rest of the day underground.

Winter Sleep

Some turtles live in places that are warm in summer, but cold in winter. Turtles rely on the sun to keep warm in summer. In winter, they need to find another way to keep warm. Some animals travel long distances to warmer places in winter. That is called migration. Most sea turtles sleep through winter. That is called **hibernation**.

As winter approaches, the turtles eat as much food as they can. Fat builds up on their body. This fat provides the turtles with energy during the winter months. As it gets colder, the turtles become sleepy. They dig a hole in the ground or in a muddy pond and settle down to hibernate.

During hibernation, the chemical composition of a turtle's blood changes so that the blood does not freeze in the cold. That helps the turtle survive in low temperatures—much lower than other hibernating creatures such as ground squirrels.

A three-toed box turtle hibernates under a bed of leaf litter.

The leatherback sea turtle might be a graceful swimmer, but it moves clumsily on land.

Giants of the Sea

The leatherback sea turtle is the largest of all the turtles. A fully grown leatherback turtle is 8 feet (2.5 m) long and weighs about 2,000 pounds (900 kg). Most turtles have hard, bony shells. The leatherback's shell is thick and leathery, which is how the turtle got its name.

Leatherbacks live in most of the world's oceans. They have a thick layer of fat under their skin, so they can survive in cold water. Leatherbacks also keep warm by closing the blood vessels that supply blood to their flippers —the turtles' paddlelike limbs. Therefore, blood is not cooled as it passes through the thin flippers. Other sea turtles can only live in warm waters or they would freeze.

Like all sea turtles, leatherbacks spend all of their life in the ocean. Only the females return to land to lay eggs. They nest on tropical beaches in the Atlantic, Indian, and Pacific Oceans.

Time to Nest

Like birds, female turtles produce their young by laying eggs. Some females nest once every few years. Others nest one or more times a year. Most females prefer to lay their eggs in the spring so the sun can keep them warm.

All turtles bury their eggs under the ground. Female turtles have a strong instinct to lay their eggs in a certain place. Leatherback sea turtles will swim for hundreds of miles to nest on the beach where they were born. Unfortunately, people have built fences and roads in many of these places. These structures prevent the females from reaching their nesting sites.

A female sea turtle crawls onto the beach to dig a nest for her clutch of eggs.

The leatherback sea
turtle lays around
100 eggs in her nest.
The eggs are the
size of billiard balls.

Moonlit Eggs

Female turtles usually lay their eggs at night when there are fewer predators around. Turtles' eggs would make a tasty meal for a fox or gull. The female starts by digging a hole with her hind limbs. When she is done, the female stands over the hole and lays her eggs.

Some turtles, such as snapping turtles, lay between 20 and 50 eggs. Some lay a single egg, while others produce several hundred eggs. The eggs are usually round, like a ball. The shell is soft and leathery, so it is unlikely to break.

When the female has finished laying her eggs, she fills the hole with sand or soil and pats it down. Some females disturb the ground around the nest, possibly in an effort to confuse predators.

Home Alone

The female turtle leaves as soon as she has laid her eggs and covered the nest. She will never see her babies hatch. It takes several months for the turtles to develop inside the eggs. That is a dangerous time. Predators may find the eggs or heavy rains could flood the nest. If the nest is not deep enough, the eggs may dry out.

If the eggs survive, the turtles will eventually be ready to hatch. Newly born turtles are called hatchlings. They have an "egg tooth" that they use to cut open their shell. As soon as the young turtle has broken free from the shell, it digs its way out of the sand.

For many species, the temperature of the nest determines the sex of the hatchlings. A warm nest results in female turtles. Male turtles emerge from a cooler nest.

The egg tooth is the small bump below the nose of this painted turtle hatchling. The egg tooth falls off after a few days.

A loggerhead hatchling crawls along the sandy beach toward the North Atlantic.

Incredible Journey

As soon as the hatchling breaks free from the egg, it crawls to the surface of the nest. Now the hatchlings must find somewhere to live. Some might need to travel a long way to find a suitable home. Amazingly, the hatchlings know exactly where they need to go. One by one, the young turtles crawl toward their destination—a pond, marsh, or the ocean.

On their incredible journey to the water, the hatchlings risk being eaten by predators such as raccoons, skunks, or seabirds. The young turtles usually hatch after dark, however, to reduce their chance of being seen.

Magnetic Sense

Sea turtles have an incredible homing device. They can spend years swimming through the oceans yet return to lay their eggs on the same exact beach where they were born.

Scientists think that turtles use Earth's magnetic field to find their way back to the nesting site. Earth's magnetic field runs from north to south. A compass needle lines up with the magnetic field to show the direction of magnetic north. How the turtles detect Earth's magnetic field remains a mystery.

Scientists think that part of the sea turtle's brain acts like a built-in compass—much like having a magnetic map of the oceans.

The alligator snapping turtle has a worm-shaped projection on the end of its tongue, which is used to lure fish to its mouth.

Little and Large

Turtle hatchlings are tiny—many would fit in the palm of an adult's hand. It is hard to believe that some of these tiny creatures grow into giant leatherback sea turtles.

The alligator snapping turtle is the biggest turtle found in North America. It weighs up to 170 pounds (76 kg) and is 31½ inches (80 cm) long—less than half the size of a leatherback sea turtle. The smallest turtle is the speckled padloper tortoise of South Africa. It is 3 inches (8 cm) long and weighs 5 ounces (140 g).

Smaller turtles can live up to five years. No one is sure exactly how long the biggest turtles can live. It could be more than 100 years. When most animals grow older, their body does not work as well as they once did. However, apart from its size, the body of a 100-year-old turtle looks the same as that of a one-year-old turtle. Turtles are unusual in the animal world because their organs **regenerate**.

Turtles at Risk

Turtles are amazing creatures that have lived on Earth for more than 200 million years. In prehistoric times, there were giant turtles—much bigger than those around now. Today, the biggest turtles in the sea are leatherbacks, and those on land are the giant tortoises found on a few islands, such as the Seychelles and the Galápagos islands. Most giant turtles disappeared from the **fossil record** when people appeared on Earth. Scientists think that people hunted the turtles for food.

Most turtles are now endangered. Sea turtles are especially at risk. As people have built beach resorts on coasts, the sea turtles have lost their nesting sites. Many species are already **extinct**.

Sea turtles are also at risk because they often come into contact with people. Big ships and fishing nets can harm sea turtles on their long migrations to warmer waters. Some people eat turtles' eggs. Others steal turtles to sell as pets. Fortunately, many organizations work to protect turtles so that future generations will be able to enjoy these amazing animals.

Words to Know

Bones Hard body parts that join up to form the skeleton inside an animal.

Carapace The top part of a turtle's shell.

Carnivores Animals that eat other animals.

Extinct No longer found on Earth.

Fossil record The discovery of extinct species whose remains are locked up inside rocks.

Herbivores Animals that only eat plants.

Hibernation A period of deep sleep during the winter to save energy.

Mammals Warm-blooded animals whose skin is covered with hair.

Musk A smelly substance produced by some animals.

49

Omnivores	Animals that eat any type of food.
Plastron	The bottom part of a turtle's shell.
Predators	Animals that hunt other animals.
Regenerate	To regrow or renew a body part.
Reptiles	Cold-blooded animals with thick skin and no fur. Crocodiles, lizards, snakes, and turtles are reptiles.
Scutes	Tough, scaly plates on a turtle's shell.
Skin	The protective outer layer that covers the body of most animals.
Species	The word used to describe animals of the same type that breed together.
Terrapins	Turtles that live in freshwater.
Tortoises	Turtles that live only on land.

Find Out More

Books

Cussen, S. and D. M. Dennis. *Those Terrific Turtles.* Sarasota, Florida: Pineapple Press, Inc., 2006.

Lasky, K. and C. G. Knight. *Interrupted Journey: Saving Endangered Sea Turtles.* Cambridge, Massachusetts: Candlewick Press, 2006.

Web sites

Aquatic Turtles
octopus.gma.org/turtles/index.html
Have fun learning about the different species of turtles with stories and activities.

Turtles and Tortoises
www.enchantedlearning.com/subjects/turtle
Facts about turtles and tortoises, including printouts.

Index